AF338129

THE STORY OF SAINT CONSTANTINE

Biography for Kids

Children's Biography Books

BABY PROFESSOR

EDUCATION KIDS

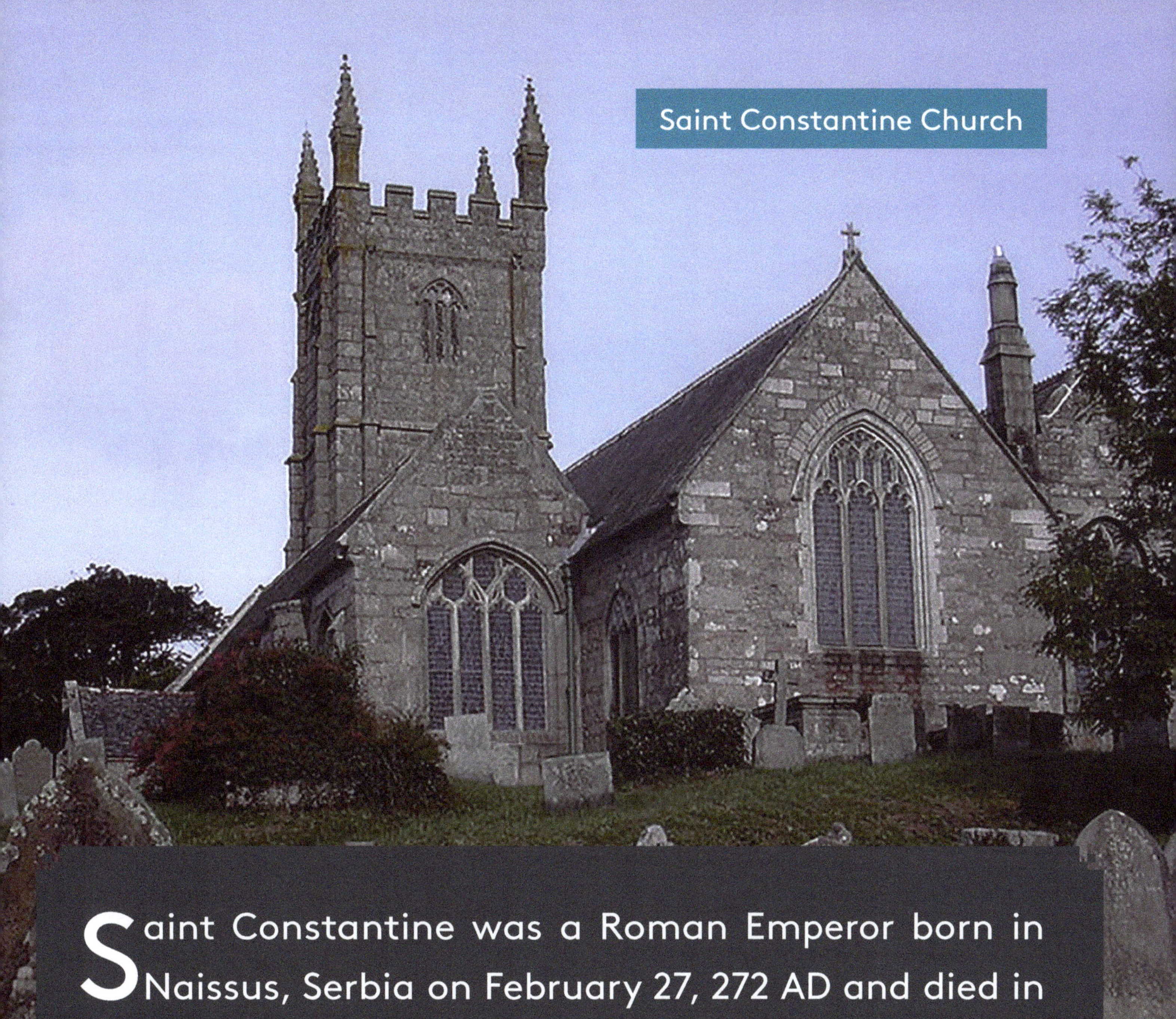

Saint Constantine was a Roman Emperor born in Naissus, Serbia on February 27, 272 AD and died in Nicomedia, Turkey on May 22, 337 AD. He was named at birth Flavius Valerius Constantinus.

He was known as the original Roman Emperor that converted to Christianity and established the city Of Constantinople. He is also referred to as Constantine the Great and Constantine I. Read further to learning more about his life and his death.

City of Constantinople

Roman Provinces

MOESIA SUPERIOR

MOESIA INFERIOR

DARDANIA

TRIBALLI

MACEDONIA

THRACIA

DACIA

PAEONIA

Acumincum
Argidava
Aquae Herculis
Burridava
Rusidava
SEN.
Taurunum
Apus
Aquae
Pincum
Tierna
Pons Traiani
Drobetae
Amutria
Acidava
Tiasum
PHIPHIGI
Lederata
Viminacium
Cuppae
Novae
Amatria
Romula
CIAGISI?
Apiaria
Municipium
Taliata
Egeta
Pulonda
Pelendava
Potula
Sectorisca
Prista
Idimum
Aquae
Transmarisca
Dorticum
Bononia
Almus
Oescus
Novae
Trimammium
Horreum Margi
Ratiaria
Gabrus
Augustae
Iatrum
MOESIA
Praes. Dasmini
Praes. Pompei
Timacum min.
Melta
Nicopolis ad Istrum
CRO.
Naissus
Remesiana
Turres
Meldia
Serdica (Ulpia)
Sub radices
Tyle
Cabyle
Scupi
Vindenis
Telanis
Scomius M.
SERDI
Bagaraca
CORALLI
Deret
Ulpiana
Lissac
Beroea
Scardus M.
AGRIANES
Pautalia
Bessapara
Hebrus
Dunax M.
DENTHE-LETAE
Philippopolis
(Trimontium)
Arzus
ODRY
Hadria
Bylazora
MAEDI
Nicopolis
Burdipta
BENNI
Astibus
Orbelus M.
Rhodope M.
COELETAE
THRAC
Stobi
Doberus
SATRAE
TRAUSI
CORPILI
PAET
PAEONIA
SINTI
Nestus
Porsulae
Plotinopolis
DEURIOPES
ODOMANTI
Sirrhae
Philippi
Sapaei
Abdera
CICONES
Trajanopolis
Ypsela
Pelagonia
Heraclea
Bora M.
Aegae
Crenides
Maronia
Lynces
Pella
EDONES
Pangaeus M.
Amphipolis
Thasus
Arcno
APSINTHII
L. Begorritis
Edessa
Bermius M.
Crestonia
Thessalonica
(Therma)
Samothrace
Callipolis
Orestis
CHALCIDICE
Pydna
Olynthus
MARE THRACICUM
Imbros
Sestus
M. Elimea
Sinus
Athos M.
Abydus

WHERE DID HE GROW UP?

He was born in Naissus approximately 272 AD. This city was located in the Roman province of Moesia, now known as Serbia. His father, Flavius Constantinus, became second in command as Caesar after working his way up the Roman government under the Emperor Diocletian.

He was raised in the Emperor Diocletian. He received an outstanding education and learned to write and read in Greek and Latin. In addition, he learned theater, mythology, and Greek philosophy. Even though he was raised in a life of privilege, in different ways he was held hostage by Emperor Diocletian to ensure his father would remain loyal.

Diocletian's Palace

Holy Land, Jerusalem

HIS FAMILY

Constantine directed Helena, his mother, to go to the Holy Land where she was able to discover some remnants of the cross that Jesus had been crucified on. Early in 326 he ordered that Fausta, his wife, and Crispus, his son be put to death.

HIS EARLY CAREER

He served as a part of the Roman army for many years. In addition, he watched Diocletian's murder and persecution of the Christians. Observing this massacre affected him for a long time.

One Diocletian became ill, he proceeded to name Galerius to be his heir. Since Galerius felt that Constantine's father was a rival, this made Constantine fear for his life. Some reports indicate that while Galerius attempted to kill him by different methods, Constantine managed to survive these attempts on his life.

Constantine was eventually able to flee and join his father in Gaul, located in the Western Roman Empire. He proceeded to spend a year fighting along with his father.

Constantius Chlorus

Constantine the Great
Y THIS SIGN CONQUER

BECOMING EMPEROR

Once his father fell ill, Constantine was named Emperor of the Roman Empire's western lands. He then became ruler of Spain, Gaul, and Britain. He then started building up and strengthening much of this area, which including building cities and roadways. His rule then moved to Trier, located in Gault, and proceeded to strengthen this city's power and also built public buildings.

He started conquering the kings around him with his huge army. The portion of this Roman Empire under his rule was expanded. People starting viewing him as a great leader. He was also able to stop the harassment of Christians living in his area.

First church commissioned by Constantine

Maxentius

THE CIVIL WAR

Once Galerius passed away around 311 AD, many of the stronger men decided that they wanted to rule over the Roman Empire and a civil war ensued. Maxentius proceeded to declare himself as Rome's new Emperor. He resided in Rome, then gained control of Italy and Rome. Constantine, along with his army then marched against him.

HE HAS A DREAM

In 312, as he approached Rome, he became increasingly worried. His army was only half of the size of Maxentius' army. Constantine experienced a dream the night before he was to face Maxentius. During this dream, he was advised he could win this battle if he was able to fight under the Christian Cross sign. On the following day, he directed his soldiers to paint a cross on their shields. They proceeded to dominate this battle, and defeated Maxentius, thus taking over control of Rome.

Remains of the Basilica of Maxentius and Constantine

Arch of Constantine

Some reports indicate that during this dream he did not see the cross, but rather saw Chi and Rho, which are Greek letters that represent Christ in the Greek language.

BECOMING A CHRISTIAN

Once he took control of Rome, he then established a coalition in the east with Licinius. During 313, the Edict of Milan was signed, stating that the Roman Empire could no longer persecute the Christians. He now deemed himself as a supporter of the Christian faith.

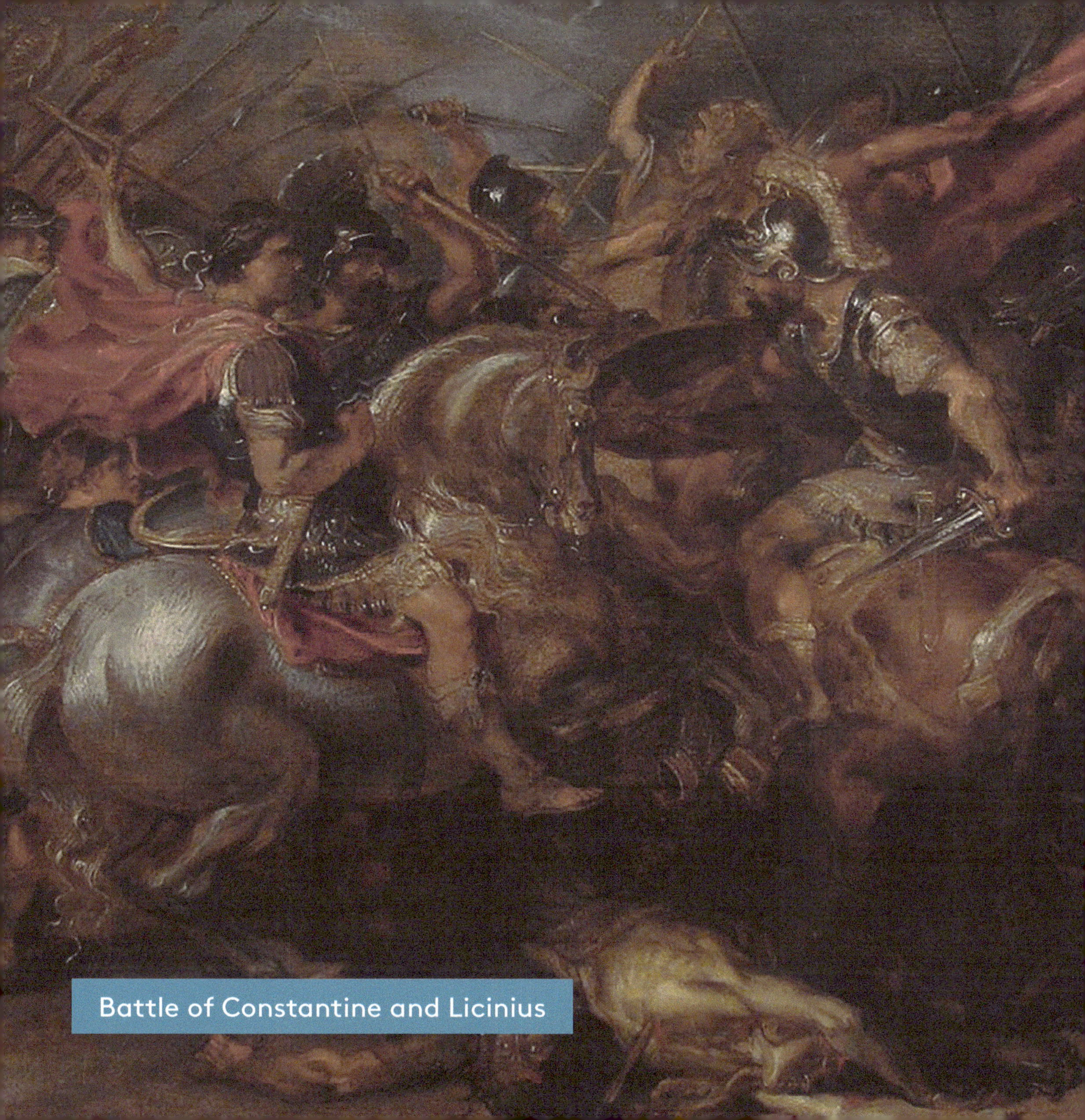
Battle of Constantine and Licinius

Baptism of Constantine

His closest mentors consisted of bishops such as Lactantius, Hosius, and Eusebius of Caesarea. He selected a group of Christians that had converted to high ranks in this Empire. These Christian ministers had special privileges and he extended several benefits to pagan priests that converted to Christian ministers. One such example would be that they would receive money from the Empire and did not have to pay taxes.

These bishops were faithful as army, but other than the creation of temples, laws and his show of support for this increasing group of priests, he didn't appear much of a Christian. He was in agreement with bishops' recommendations to enact laws against this magic and private divination. However, if no changes occurred in these types of laws by an influential bishop, he had no interest in attempting to make these changes.

Temple of Aphrodite

With Constantine's decree, most of the pagan temples were demolished. For instance, he ordered that the Temple of Aphrodite in London be damaged, as well as several other ceremonial pagan locations. It seemed to be that his interested was in destroying some of the pre-Christian cult locations, however, they were not all to be destroyed.

In each decision to destroy one, it was noted that it couldn't exist as it had been the home of misguided ceremonies and rites, a location of true obstinacy. While he did not ban these rituals outright, he did close and destroyed the more important temples once the bishops decided they were dangerous to their faith.

Saint Constantine & Elena church

Arch of Constantine

Other than Constantine's political motives supporting the growth in the army of priests, he may have had a secret. Even more interesting, it seems that Rome's bishop knew of it, and supported him. The truth became evident that he seemingly supported this newer religion, but still worshipped the Sun and the pagan symbols.

He was raised in the court of the emperor Constantine Chlorus. Emperor Chlorus was a Neoplatonist and was devoted to the Unconquered Sun. Empress Helena, who was his mother, was a Christian travelling the Middle East in search of key locations related to Jesus.

Helena

Ancient texts reveal that she was the person that was able to identify the more important locations known in the Bible. As a youngster, Constantine did not appear to follow the religious interests of his mother. He was known to worship the Sun, a devotee of Mithraism.

In 312, after he was officially converted to Christianity, he built the triumphal arch in Rome. It seems interesting that this arch was not dedicated to Christianity symbols, but rather to the Unconquered Sun. During Constantine's reign, he was able to change several aspects relating to the pagan cults, but this did not mean that he was able to stop the cultivations of the older traditions.

He would give them different names, but would allow for the pagan practices to continue in several ways. In 321, for example, he enacted a law that celebrated the Day of the Sun be a state holiday, which meant a day off for all.

EMPEROR OF ROME

Licinius made a decision seven years later to again begin the persecuting the Christians. Constantine did not like this and then decided to march against Licinius. After many battles, he defeated Licinius and in 324 became the ruler of Rome, which was now united.

Battle between the Fleets of Constantine and Licinius

The Basilica of Constantine and Maxentius

BUILDING ROME

He built several structures, including an enormous basilica located in the forum, leaving his mark on Rome. He also remodeled the Circus Maximus so that it could hold more people. His most notable building might be the Arch of Constantine, which is located in Rome. In addition, he had a massive arch built to memorialize his triumph over Maxentius.

CONSTANTINOPLE

He established the new capital of this Empire in 330 AD. It was built in the ancient city of Byzantium. It was named Constantinople after the Constantine the Emperor and later became the Eastern Roman Empire capitol, also referred to as the Byzantine Empire.

Constantinople

DEATH

Constantine was not baptized as Christian until just prior to passing away. Until he passed away in 337, he ruled this Empire. He was then laid to rest in Constantinople at the Church of the Holy Apostles.

Constantinople was the richest and the largest city until falling to the Ottoman Empire in 1453. It is now known as Istanbul, Turkey's capital.

Constantinople, Turkey

CONSTANTINE, BY TH

CHRISTIAN, GOD, OR PAGAN

After he died, he became a pagan god. An examination of the archaeological sites implies that he, similar to other Roman emperors, never ceased to see himself to be son of the ancient deities. It's difficult to believe that his Christian beliefs were strong like those of his mother, Helena. He seems to be more of an intellectual politician than someone that truly desired to Christianize the world.

For additional information about Constantine the Great and Ancient Rome, be sure to research the internet, go to your local library, and ask questions of your teachers, family and friends.

Old Jerusalem

Visit

BABY PROFESSOR
EDUCATION KIDS

www.BabyProfessorBooks.com
to download Free Baby Professor eBooks
and view our catalog of new and exciting
Children's Books